Gray

by Iain Gray

79 Main Street, Newtongrange,
Midlothian EH22 4NA
Tel: 0131 344 0414
E-mail: info@lang-syne.co.uk
www.langsyneshop.co.uk

Design by Dorothy Meikle
Printed by Printwell Ltd
© Lang Syne Publishers Ltd 2022

All rights reserved. No part of this publication may be reproduced, stored or introduced into a retrieval system, or transmitted in any form or by any means (electronic, mechanical, photocopying, recording or otherwise) without the prior written permission of Lang Syne Publishers Ltd.

ISBN 978-1-85217-586-3

Gray

MOTTO:
Anchor, fast anchor.

CREST:
An anchor.

NAME variations include:
- Graye
- Grays
- Grey
- Groy

Chapter one:

The origins of popular surnames

by George Forbes and Iain Gray

***If you don't know where you came from, you won't know where you're going* is a frequently quoted observation and one that has a particular resonance today when there has been a marked upsurge in interest in genealogy, with increasing numbers of people curious to trace their family roots.**

Main sources for genealogical research include census returns and official records of births, marriages and deaths – and the key to unlocking the detail they contain is obviously a family surname, one that has been 'inherited' and passed from generation to generation.

No matter our station in life, we all have a surname – but it was not until about the middle of the fourteenth century that the practice of being identified by a particular surname became commonly established throughout the British Isles.

Previous to this, it was normal for a person to be identified through the use of only a forename.

But as population gradually increased and there were many more people with the same forename, surnames were adopted to distinguish one person, or community, from another.

Many common English surnames are patronymic in origin, meaning they stem from the forename of one's father – with 'Johnson,' for example, indicating 'son of John.'

It was the Normans, in the wake of their eleventh century conquest of Anglo-Saxon England, a pivotal moment in the nation's history, who first brought surnames into usage – although it was a gradual process.

For the Normans, these were names initially based on the title of their estates, local villages and chateaux in France to distinguish and identify these landholdings.

Such grand descriptions also helped enhance the prestige of these warlords and generally glorify their lofty positions high above the humble serfs slaving away below in the pecking order who had only single names, often with Biblical connotations as in Pierre and Jacques.

The only descriptive distinctions among the peasantry concerned their occupations, like 'Pierre the swineherd' or 'Jacques the ferryman.'

Roots of surnames that came into usage in England not only included Norman-French, but also Old French, Old Norse, Old English, Middle English, German, Latin, Greek, Hebrew and the Gaelic languages of the Celts.

The Normans themselves were originally Vikings, or 'Northmen', who raided, colonised and eventually settled down around the French coastline.

They had sailed up the Seine in their longboats in 900AD under their ferocious leader Rollo and ruled the roost in north eastern France before sailing over to conquer England in 1066 under Duke William of Normandy – better known to posterity as William the Conqueror, or King William I of England.

Granted lands in the newly-conquered England, some of their descendants later acquired territories in Wales, Scotland and Ireland – taking not only their own surnames, but also the practice of adopting a surname, with them.

But it was in England where Norman rule and custom first impacted, particularly in relation to the adoption of surnames.

This is reflected in the famous *Domesday Book*, a massive survey of much of England and Wales, ordered by William I, to determine who owned what, what it was worth and therefore how much they were liable to pay in taxes to the voracious Royal Exchequer.

Completed in 1086 and now held in the National Archives in Kew, London, 'Domesday' was an Old English word meaning 'Day of Judgement.'

This was because, in the words of one contemporary chronicler, "its decisions, like those of the Last Judgement, are unalterable."

It had been a requirement of all those English landholders – from the richest to the poorest – that they identify themselves for the purposes of the survey and for future reference by means of a surname.

This is why the *Domesday Book*, although written in Latin as was the practice for several centuries with both civic and ecclesiastical records, is an invaluable source for the early appearance of a wide range of English surnames.

Several of these names were coined in connection with occupations.

These include Baker and Smith, while Cooks, Chamberlains, Constables and Porters were to be found carrying out duties in large medieval households.

The church's influence can be found in names such as Bishop, Friar and Monk while the popular name of Bennett derives from the late fifth to mid-sixth century Saint Benedict, founder of the Benedictine order of monks.

The early medical profession is represented by Barber, while businessmen produced names that include Merchant and Sellers.

Down at the village watermill, the names that cropped up included Millar/Miller, Walker and Fuller, while other self-explanatory trades included Cooper, Tailor, Mason and Wright.

Even the scenery was utilised as in Moor, Hill, Wood and Forrest – while the hunt and the chase supplied names that include Hunter, Falconer, Fowler and Fox.

Colours are also a source of popular surnames, as in Black, Brown, Gray/Grey, Green and White, and would have denoted the colour of the clothing the person habitually wore or, apart from the obvious exception of 'Green', one's hair colouring or even complexion.

The surname Red developed into Reid, while

Blue was rare and no-one wanted to be associated with yellow.

Rather self-important individuals took surnames that include Goodman and Wiseman, while physical attributes crept into surnames such as Small and Little.

Many families proudly boast the heraldic device known as a Coat of Arms, as featured on our front cover.

The central motif of the Coat of Arms would originally have been what was borne on the shield of a warrior to distinguish himself from others on the battlefield.

Not featured on the Coat of Arms, but highlighted on page three, is the family motto and related crest – with the latter frequently different from the central motif.

Adding further variety to the rich cultural heritage that is represented by surnames is the appearance in recent times in lists of the 100 most common names found in England of ones that include Khan, Patel and Singh – names that have proud roots in the vast sub-continent of India.

Echoes of a far distant past can still be found in our surnames and they can be borne with pride in commemoration of our forebears.

Chapter two:

Of high degree

A name of ancient roots, 'Gray' and its popular spelling variant of 'Grey' has a number of possible points of origin.

One is that it derives from the Old English 'graeg', descriptive of someone who had grey hair, a grey beard or habitually wore grey-coloured clothing, while it is also a locational name.

Some sources assert the first bearer of the name was the Norman Fulbert de Croy – with 'Croy' a French form of 'Gray' – who took his name from the lands of Croy in Picardy.

Great Chamberlain to Robert, Duke of Normandy, who granted him the lands, he is reputed to have been the father of Arlotta, the mother of Duke William of Normandy who is better known to posterity as William the Conqueror.

Some sources state the name first came to England in the form of Anchetil de Greye, who accompanied Duke William in the Norman Invasion of England in 1066.

Anchetil de Greye – with 'Anchetil' derived

from a Norse form of 'God-Cauldron' – is believed to have taken his surname from his estate of what today is Graye-sur-Mer, in Calvados.

As reward for his services to William, who usurped the Anglo-Saxon monarchy to become England's William I, he was granted the estate of Redrefield – later known as Rotherfield Greys – and the manor house now known as Grey's Court in South Oxfordshire.

His descendants also came to possess lands in West Oxfordshire and in Kent, but it is with Northumberland, in the far north of England, that the Grays/Greys came to be particularly identified.

A vast area, Northumberland was for centuries a blood-soaked battleground for feuding English and Scottish Borders' clans and also warring armies; in Scotland and Ireland, the Gray/Grey name was also found as an Anglicisation of the Gaelic 'riabach.'

Anchetil de Greye, meanwhile, was the great-grandfather of John de Gray, the Bishop of Durham who was a trusted advisor of John, who reigned as King of England from 1199 to 1216.

His date and place of birth are not known, but what is known is that it was as reward for his services to John that in 1200 he was granted the lucrative and powerful post of Bishop of Norwich.

As further reward, the King in 1205 attempted to have him recognised as Archbishop of Canterbury – but Pope Innocent III refused to recognise the appointment, in favour of Stephen Langton.

Appointed Governor of Ireland in 1209, he died in 1214 only a few days after being appointed Bishop of Durham.

His nephew Walter de Gray also held high office. Born in Norfolk in about 1180, the son of John de Gray the Elder, of Eaton, it was through his uncle's influence with King John that he first rose to prominence.

Appointed Lord Chancellor of England in 1205 and later Bishop of Lichfield and then Bishop of Worcester, he was present in 1215 at Runnymede, beside the River Thames, in Surrey, when John signed the famous charter of English civil liberties known as the *Magna Carta – Great Charter* – an act that had been forced on him by his disaffected and powerful barons.

Following John's death a year later, Walter de Gray acted as a royal official during the minority of Henry III.

Later appointed Archbishop of York he was responsible for building the south transept of York Minster and buying the village of Bishopthorpe, which became the official residence of the Archbishop of York; he died in 1255.

Another descendant of Anchetil de Greye was the soldier and courtier John de Grey, 1st Baron Grey de Rotherfield.

Born in 1300 and serving as Lord Steward of the Royal Household of Edward III, he was one of the founding members in 1348 of The Most Noble Order of the Garter – which today survives as the highest order of chivalry in the United Kingdom and the Commonwealth and is dedicated to St George, England's patron saint.

Membership of the exclusive Order is awarded at the ruling monarch's pleasure and, with its motto of *Honi soit qui mal y pense – Shame on him who thinks evil of it* – membership is limited, apart from the monarch and the Prince of Wales, to no more than 24 'Companions' at a time.

Back in the early Gray/Grey heartland of present-day Northumberland, Sir Thomas Grey, born in 1384 at Castle Heaton, near Norham, was along with Henry Scrope, 3rd Baron Scrope of Masham and

Richard Conisburgh, 3rd Earl of Cambridge, executed for their role in an abortive attempt to assassinate King Henry V.

Known as the Southampton Plot, the plan had been to assassinate the king before he boarded ship at Southampton for France and replace him on the throne with Edmund Mortimer, 3rd Earl of March.

Hopelessly incompetent in their planning, the plot was revealed to the king in July of 1415 and Grey and his fellow conspirators duly beheaded at the North Gate of Southampton the following month.

A half-brother of King Edward V through his mother Elizabeth Woodville, Sir Richard Grey was the knight who also fell victim to the complex family and political machinations of his time.

Born in 1457, his father Sir John de Grey of Groby was killed during the tumultuous period known as the Wars of the Roses fighting for the House of Lancaster against the rival House of York at the second battle of St Albans in February of 1461.

Suspected of having entertained his own ambitions to the throne following the succession of his half-brother and, later, by Richard, Duke of Gloucester as Richard III, he was executed at Pontefract Castle in June of 1483.

One particularly tragic bearer of the name was Lady Jane Grey, also known as Lady Jane Dudley and, to posterity, as "The Nine Days' Queen."

Born in 1536, a great-grand-daughter of Henry VII through his younger daughter Mary and a first cousin once removed of Edward VI, it was in 1553 that she married Lord Guildford Dudley, younger son of John Dudley, Duke of Northumberland.

When she was aged only 15, the dying Edward VI nominated her as his successor – subverting the claims to the throne of his half-sisters Mary and Elizabeth.

Despite his dying wish, the hapless Jane was imprisoned in the Tower of London for a time.

In the complex faction fighting of the age, she was released and proclaimed Queen – reigning only from July 10 of 1553 until July 19 when she was convicted of high treason and sentenced to death by the Privy Council which had switched its allegiance to Mary.

Also convicted of treason, her husband was publicly executed at Tower Hill, outside the Tower, while Jane was subjected to the gruesome ordeal of being beheaded at Tower Green, inside the Tower, in February of 1554.

Others who fell victim to the executioner's axe after having been found guilty of treason by usurping the throne were Edward Stanley, 3rd Earl of Derby and John Bourchier, 2nd Earl of Bath.

Yet another tragic figure was Lady Jane Grey's younger sister, Lady Catherine Grey, also known as Catherine Seymour, Countess of Hereford.

Born in 1540, it was in 1560 that she incurred the vicious wrath of Elizabeth, who had succeeded Mary on the throne, by marrying one of her favourites, Edward Seymour, 1st Earl of Hereford.

Based on totally unfounded suspicions that Catherine and her husband had designs on the throne, they were officially censured as "fornicators" and, deemed guilty of "carnal copulation", their marriage was annulled by the Archbishop of Canterbury.

This ensured that Catherine and her two young sons were now ineligible to take up the throne.

Placed under what today would be termed 'house arrest', she died in 1568 from consumption.

In later years, both she and her husband were reunited in death by being re-interred together in Salisbury Cathedral.

Chapter three:

Science and invention

In later centuries, bearers of the Gray and Grey names have achieved fame through decidedly more peaceful endeavours and pursuits, not least in the sciences.

Born in 1748, Edward Whitaker Gray was the English physician, botanist and zoologist noted as having been a keeper of the natural history and antiquities department of the British Museum, London; author of the highly detailed 1791 *Catalogue of Shells*, he died in 1806.

He was the uncle of Samuel Frederick Gray, the noted botanist, mycologist and pharmacologist born in London in 1766.

Author of pioneering reference works that include his 1823 *The Operative Chemist*, he died in 1828, while he was also the author seven years before his death of *The Natural Arrangement of British Plants*.

On American shores, Asa Gray was the nineteenth century botanist celebrated as having methodically and tirelessly classified the vast majority of the plants of North America.

Born in 1810 in Sauquoit, New York, it was after having been appointed the first professor of botany and zoology at the University of Michigan and later professor of natural history at Harvard University, that he published works that include the grandly titled *Manual of the Botany of the Northern United States, from New England to Wisconsin and south to Ohio and Pennsylvania Inclusive*.

With illustrations by Isaac Sprague and more popularly, and briefly, known simply as *Gray's Manual*, it remains a classic of the genre to this day.

He died in 1888, while Gray's Peak, in Colorado, is named in his honour and the Asa Gray Award is awarded by the American Society of Plant Taxonomists to honour botanists.

The U.S. Postal Service issued an Asa Gray postage stamp in his honour in 2011 as part of its *American Scientists* collection.

In the world of engineering, Thomas Lomar Gray was the Scottish engineer who, along with James Alfred Ewing and John Milne, carried out pioneering work in seismology.

Born in 1850 in Lochgelly, Fife and a graduate in engineering from Glasgow University, it was while he was working with Ewing and Milne at the Imperial College of Engineering in Tokyo, Japan that between 1880 and 1895 he developed the first seismometers to detect earthquake activity.

Later professor of dynamic engineering at what is now the Rose-Hullman Institute of Technology in Terre Haute, Indiana, he died in 1908.

In the abstract world of higher mathematics, Alfred Gray, born in 1939 in Dallas, Texas, was the leading American mathematician renowned for his work in the fields of differential geometry and differential equations.

Professor of mathematics at Maryland University, he died in 1998.

During the Second World War, Nigel de Gray was the code-breaker who, working from the highly secret British code-breaking facility at Bletchley Park, Buckinghamshire, was part of the team who decrypted German radio traffic through the Enigma cypher machine.

Born in 1886 in Copdock, Suffolk and a descendant of the 5th Lord Walsingham, he had also been responsible during the First World War for decrypting the *Zimmerman Telegram*.

This was a telegram from the German Foreign Secretary Arthur Zimmerman to the German ambassador in Mexico instructing him to offer military aid to help them 'take' the American states of Arizona, New Texas and New Mexico in return for Mexico siding with Germany in the war.

It was the revelation of this telegram that proved a major factor in the previously 'isolationist' United States entering the war against Germany; later working as a deputy director of GCHQ in Cheltenham, Gray died in 1951.

In the world of medicine, Henry Gray, born in 1827 and who died in 1861, was the English surgeon and anatomist famous for the medical textbook *Gray's Anatomy*.

Known as 'The Bible of Anatomy', seven editions were published between 1860 and 1880 alone, while a 40th edition was published in 2008 to mark the 150th anniversary of its first publication.

In the world of contemporary politics, Iain Gray is the Scottish Labour Party politician, born in 1957, who served as leader of his party as Member of the Scottish Parliament (MSP) for East Lothian from September of 2008 until December of 2011.

In nineteenth century politics, Charles Grey, 2nd Earl Grey and Viscount Howick of Howick Hall, Northumberland, born in 1764, served as the British

Whig Party Prime Minister from November of 1830 until July of 1834.

A leading advocate of Parliamentary reform and instrumental in the passage of the landmark Reform Act of 1832, he died in 1845, while he also lends his name to the tea blend known as Earl Grey.

A blend of citrus flavour derived from oil extracted from the rind of bergamot orange, it is complemented by the equally noted blend of Lady Grey, named for his wife.

In the artistic world, Effie Gray, born Euphemia Chalmers Gray in Perth, Scotland, in 1828 and later better known as Lady Millais, was the wife of the famed Pre-Raphaelite painter John Everett Millais.

She was the subject of an unusual love triangle, when, after marrying the author and literary critic John Ruskin, she separated from him to marry Millais.

According to accounts, Effie and Ruskin never actually consummated their marriage – although Ruskin was deeply in love with her – and their marriage was annulled in 1854.

Marrying Millais a year after the annulment

and the subject of a number of his paintings, she died in 1897.

Buried in Kinnoul Churchyard, Perthshire and the inspiration for Millais' poignant painting *The Vale of Rest*, she has been the subject of a number of literary works and films that include the 2013 film *Effie*, produced by Emma Thompson and with Dakota Fleming in the title role.

Chapter four:

On the world stage

Best known for her role from 1978 to 1989 of Sue Ellen in the television drama series *Dallas*, Linda Gray is the American actress, producer and former model born Linda Ann Gray in Santa Monica, California, in 1940.

It was for her portrayal of Sue Ellen, long-suffering wife of oil tycoon J.R. Ewing, that she was the recipient of a Primetime Emmy Award for Outstanding Lead Actress in a Drama Serial and nominated for two Golden Globe Awards for Best Actress – Television Series Drama.

Other credits include the television movies *Moment of Truth: Why My Daughter*, the 1996 *Dallas: J.R. Returns* and, from 1998, *Dallas: War of the Ewings*.

Also an accomplished stage actress, she starred in London's West End and on Broadway as Mrs Robinson in a 2001 production of *The Graduate*, while in 2007 she toured the United Kingdom in a production of *Terms of Endearment*.

Born in Bournemouth in 1928, **Charles Gray**

was the veteran English actor born Donald Marshall Gray and who is best known for his role of the villainous Blofeld in the 1971 James Bond film *Diamonds Are Forever*.

Other Bond movie credits include the 1967 *You Only Live Twice*, while he is also known for his role of Sherlock Holmes' brother Mycroft in the television series *The Adventures of Sherlock Holmes*.

With other television credits that include the cult classic *The Prisoner* and also known for his role of the criminologist in *The Rocky Horror Picture Show*, he died in 2000.

Winner of an Academy Award for Best Supporting Actor for his portrayal of the master of ceremonies in the 1972 film version of the musical *Cabaret*, **Joel Grey** is the American actor, singer and dancer born Joel David Katz in 1932.

Winner of a Tony Award for his role in the 1966 Broadway production of *Cabaret*, other stage credits include the 1962 *Stop the World – I Want to Get Off*, the 2003 *Wicked* and, from 2011, *Anything Goes*.

Formerly married to the actress and singer Jo Wilder, he is the father of the actress **Jennifer Grey**, born in New York City in 1960.

Nominated for a Golden Globe Award for her portrayal, opposite the late Patrick Swayze, of Francis "Baby" Houseman in the 1987 film *Dirty Dancing*, other screen credits include the 1984 *Reckless* and, from 1986, *Ferris Bueller's Day Off*.

With television credits that include *Maverick*, *Alfred Hitchcock Presents*, *Perry Mason*, *77 Sunset Strip* and *Bonanza*, **Coleen Gray** is the American actress born Doris Jensen in 1922 in Staplehurst, Nebraska.

Major big screen credits include the 1947 *Nightmare Alley*, starring with Tyrone Power, the 1948 *Red River*, opposite John Wayne and, from 1956, *The Killing*.

Not only an actress of stage, television and the big screen but also an author and a lepidopterist, **Dulcie Gray** was born Dulcie Winifred Catherine Bailey in 1915 in what was then British Malaya – now Malaysia.

Married from 1939 to fellow English actor Michael Dennison, she starred in a number of films beside him that include the 1948 *The Glass Mountain* and *My Brother Jonathan* and, from 1952, *Angels One Five*.

Also known for her television role in the

drama series *Howard's Way*, as an author she penned the *Inspector Cardiff* series of crime novels while, as a lepidopterist, she wrote *Butterflies on My Mind*; the recipient of a CBE, she died in 2011.

Married in 1949 to the English entertainer Brian Rix, **Elspet Gray**, more formally known as Baroness Rix, was the Scottish actress born in 1929.

Best known for television roles that include that of Lady Collingford in the children's series *Catweazle*, the comedy series *Solo*, where she starred beside Felicity Kendal and as Hilary in the sitcom *Dinnerladies*, she died in 2013.

Through her husband Brian Rix, chairman for a time of the mental health charity Mencap and who was ennobled as a life peer in 1992, she was the mother of the actress **Louisa Rix** and the author **Jamie Rix**.

Born in 1955, Louisa has credits that include that of 'Kevin's Mum' in the *Harry Enfield* television series and the 2000 film *Kevin and Perry Go Large*, while her brother Jamie, born in 1959, is the author of books that include his 1990 *Grizzly Tales for Gruesome Kids*.

Ranked in 1975 as one of America's top models and the 'face' of beauty products that included

Max Factor and L'Oreal, **Erin Gray** is the American actress born in 1950 in Honolulu, Hawaii and whose credits include the television series *Buck Rogers in the 25th Century* and the sitcom *Silver Spoons*.

Grandly known as Constance Vera Browne, Baroness Oranmore and Browne, **Sally Gray** was the English actress of the 1930s and 1940s whose many film credits include the 1941 *Dangerous Moonlight*, the 1946 *Green for Danger* and, from 1952, *Escape Route*.

Born in 1916 and married to the Anglo-Irish peer the 4th Baron Oronmore and Browne, she died in 2006.

On British television screens, **Andy Gray** is the Scottish actor and comedy writer born in 1960.

Acting and writing credits include *Naked Video*, while he is also known for his role of Chancer in the 1987 sitcom *City Lights*, starring beside the late Gerard Kelly; other television credits include *Two Thousand Acres of Sky* and, from 2007, *Legit*.

Back on American shores, Dolores Stein, born in Chicago in 1924 and who died in 2002, was the actress and singer better known by her stage name of **Dolores Gray**.

Performing the lead role in 1949 in the first

London West End stage production of *Annie Get Your Gun* and winner of a Tony Award for Best Lead Actress in a Musical for her role in the 1953 production of *Carnival in Flanders*, she also sang Marilyn Monroe's part on the soundtrack album for the 1954 film *There's No Business Like Show Business*.

Behind the camera lens, **James Gray**, born in 1969 in New York City, is the film director and screenwriter whose credits include the 1994 *Little Odessa*, starring Tim Roth, and winner of the Silver Lion Award at the Venice Film Festival; other credits include *The Immigrant*, nominated for the Palme d'Or at the 2013 Cannes Film Festival.

Bearers of the Gray and Grey names have also excelled in the highly competitive world of sport.

Born in 1969 in Cardiff, Carys Davina Grey is the award-winning disabled former athlete better known as **Tanni Grey-Thompson**.

The name 'Tanni' comes from when her older sister first referred to her as 'tiny' when she first saw her, but pronounced it 'tanni.'

The name stuck, and it was as Tanni Grey-Thompson – married to the research chemist and former wheelchair athlete Dr Ian Thompson – that she achieved fame by winning a clutch of medals that include a gold for both the 100-metres and 400-metres wheelchair race at the 2004 Paralympic Games in Athens.

The recipient of an MBE and a CBE for her services to sport, she was elevated to the Peerage of the United Kingdom in 2005 as a Dame Commander of the Order of the British Empire (DBE), giving her the title of Baroness Grey-Thompson.

On the fields of European football, Edwin Gray, born in Glasgow in 1948 and better known as **Eddie Gray**, is the Scottish winger who was a star of English club Leeds United in the 1960s and 1970s.

Voted in 2000 as the third greatest Leeds United player of all time, he is also an inductee of the English Football Hall of Fame.

Born in Glasgow in 1955, Andrew Mullen Gray, better known as **Andy Gray**, is the Scottish former footballer who, in addition to playing for his national team, also played for clubs that include Dundee United, Aston Villa, Wolverhampton Wanderers and Rangers; he is now a football pundit.

From sport to the world of music, **David Gray** is the internationally successful singer and songwriter, born in 1968 in Sale, Manchester, who has enjoyed success with singles such as *Babylon*, taken from his 2000 album *White Ladder*.

Not only a top-selling singer and songwriter but also an actress and record producer, Natalie Renée McIntyre, born in 1969 in Canton, Ohio, is better known by her stage name of **Macy Gray**.

Albums include her 1999 debut *On How Life Is*, while her 2001 single *I Try* won a Grammy Award for Best Female Pop Vocal performance.

Films in which she has appeared include the 2001 *Training Day*, the 2002 *Spider-Man* and the 2010 *Colored Girls*.

Born in 1958 in Essex, **Paul Gray** is the former bass guitarist with the band Eddie and the Hot Rods and, later, punk band The Damned, while **Les Gray**, born in 1946 and who died in 2004, was the English musician best known as the vocalist with the band Mud.

From music to the equally creative world of the written word, **Spalding Gray** was the American writer and actor best known for his series of autobiographical monologues that include his *Swimming to Cambodia*, adapted for the film of the name in 1987.

Born in 1941 in Providence, Rhode Island

and also author of the 1986 *Sex and Death to the Age of 14*, he died in 2004 as a result of apparent suicide.

Author of the 1912 novel *Riders of the Purple Sage* and many other popular works in the Western' genre, **Zane Grey**, born Pearl Zane Grey in 1872, was the American author whose many works, including *Riders of the Purple Sage*, were adapted for film; he died in 1939.

Not only an accomplished Scottish award-winning writer but also an artist, **Alasdair Gray** was born in 1934 in Riddrie, in the east end of Glasgow.

His 1981 novel *Lanark*, described as "one of the landmarks of 20th century fiction", was followed by his 1992 *Poor Things*, winner of a Whitbread Novel Award and the *Guardian* Fiction Prize.

A student at Glasgow School of Art from 1952 to 1957 and where he taught from 1958 to 1962, his many artistic murals include that for the auditorium of the Òran Mór venue in Glasgow's Byres Road, and recognised as one of the largest works of art in Scotland.

Another former pupil of Glasgow School of Art is the journalist, author and broadcaster **Muriel Gray**.

Born in 1958 in East Kilbride and the first

female chair of the school's board of governors she was a presenter, along with Jules Holland, of the former television music show *The Tube* and is the author of acclaimed horror novels that include the 1995 *The Trickster*.

Considered one of the most popular poems in the English language, *Elegy Written in a Country Churchyard*, or, simply, *Gray's Elegy*, was written by the English poet, classical scholar and history professor **Thomas Gray**, who was born in London in 1716.

The poet, who died in 1771, is buried in Stoke Poges churchyard, in Buckinghamshire, where he is believed to have written his famous poem.

Born in 1951 in Houston, Texas, **John Gray** is the American author best known for his 1992 *Men Are From Mars, Women Are From Venus*.

Having to date sold more than seven million copies, the book's title has even entered the common vernacular.